OSTRICHES

Maddie Gibbs

PowerKiDS press

New York

Published in 2011 by The Rosen Publishing Group, Inc.
29 East 21st Street, New York, NY 10010

First Edition

Editor: Amelie von Zumbusch
Layout Design: Greg Tucker

Photo Credits: Cover, pp. 5, 11, 13, 15, 19, 21, 24 (top left), 24 (top right), 24 (bottom right) Shutterstock .com; p. 7 Tom Brakefield/Stockbyte/Thinkstock; pp. 9, 17, 23, 24 (bottom left) iStockphoto/Thinkstock.

Library of Congress Cataloging-in-Publication Data

Gibbs, Maddie.
 Ostriches / by Maddie Gibbs. — 1st ed.
   p. cm. — (Safari animals)
 Includes index.
 ISBN 978-1-4488-2509-7 (library binding) — ISBN 978-1-4488-2600-1 (pbk.) —
 ISBN 978-1-4488-2601-8 (6-pack)
 1. Ostriches—Juvenile literature. I. Title.
 QL696.S9G53 2011
 598.5'24—dc22
                        2010021457

Manufactured in the United States of America

CPSIA Compliance Information: Batch #WW11PK: For Further Information contact Rosen Publishing, New York, New York at 1-800-237-9932

CONTENTS

Ostriches are the world's biggest birds. They can be up to 9 feet (3 m) tall!

5

Ostriches have long necks.
They have long legs, too.

The ostrich has the biggest eyes of any land animal. Its eyes are 2 inches (5 cm) wide.

9

Ostriches are too big to fly.
Instead, they walk or run.

Ostriches are fast. They can run faster than 40 miles per hour (64 km/h).

13

Ostriches live in Africa's deserts and **savannas**.

15

Ostriches eat many foods, such as bugs, leaves, and seeds.

Baby ostriches **hatch** from big eggs. Ostrich eggs weigh about 3 pounds (1 kg).

19

Ostrich **chicks** often follow their mothers and fathers around.

Ostriches live in groups, called **herds**. Herd members look out for one another.

Words to Know

chicks

hatch

herd

savanna

Index

Web Sites

Due to the changing nature of Internet links, PowerKids Press has developed an online list of Web sites related to the subject of this book. This site is updated regularly. Please use this link to access the list:
www.powerkidslinks.com/safari/ostrich/